Gerson Therap

MW00932572

A Healing Wonder to Cure Diseases and Restore Health by Eliminating Toxins and Boosting Immunity

Raphael Smith

Contents

Introduction

Imagine a world where you can have good health and a lot of energy. A World where the very core of nature's gifts can heal your body, refresh your mind, and make you feel better all around.

In this complete guide, we go on an amazing journey through the Gerson Therapy juice recipes, which were carefully made to help your body fix itself. From breakfast energizers to detoxifying green juices, tonics for health, elixirs of restoratives, and recipes to treat particular health problems, each chapter is a treasure trove of tasty drinks that are meant to feed and heal.

In Chapter 1, we talk about energizing Morning Energizers like the Powerful Green Juice, which is full of nutrients, and the spicy Orange-Rot Splash, which will wake you up. In Chapter 2, the Cleansing Green Juices are introduced. These include The Ultimate Detox, a powerful beverage that will clean your body, and the refreshing Green beverage, which will make you feel better from the inside out.

As we move into Chapter 3, we find Tonics for Health, such as the energizing Infrared Glow and the Immunity Booster, which is a drink that boosts your immune system.

In Chapter 4, "Recipes for Heart Health," you'll find delicious drinks like Beetroot-Celery Juice and Watermelon-Mint Juice that are good for your cardiovascular system.

In Chapter 5, "How to Cook for Healthy Kidneys," we learn how to clean the kidneys with cucumber and parsley juice and wake them up with carrot, celery, and parsley juice. In Chapter 6, "Recipes for Losing Weight," you can find recipes like "Apple-Cucumber Juice" and "Spinach, Cucumber, and Lemon Juice," which help you get rid of toxins.

In Chapter 7, "Recipes for Anti-Aging," we look at Pomegranate-Carrot Juice, which is full of antioxidants, and Blueberry-Kale Juice, which helps you feel younger. In Chapter 8, we unlock Recipes for Healthy Brains, which has drinks like Ginger-Turmeric Carrot Juice, which improves memory, and Blueberry-Beetroot Juice, which helps the brain.

Recipes for Anti-Cancer take us on a trip through Chapter 9, where we learn about the powerful Carrot-Apple-Beet Juice and the immune-boosting Grapefruit-Carrot Juice. In this guide, Chapter 10 explains the importance of juicing in the Gerson Therapy, and Chapter 11 goes over the many benefits of juice and a lot more in to be seen in other chapters.

Get ready for an adventure that will change your life as we reveal the secrets of Gerson Therapy juice. Let nature's gifts feed, heal, and refresh you from the inside out.

Chapter 1: Juice Recipes for Gerson Therapy Morning Energizers

As part of the Gerson Therapy, you can add the following invigorating juice recipes into your morning routine:

1. Powerful Green Juice:

Gerson Therapy says that drinking Powerful Green Juice helps the body become more alkaline, get more oxygen, and boost the immune system. This can help the body heal and reduce inflammation. People also think that the juice helps the liver work, helps with digestion, and makes bowel movements more likely.

Ingredients:

- 6 to 8 kale or spinach leaves

- Two stalks of celery

- One cucumber

- 1 tangerine

- 1 peeled lemon

Directions:

1. Thoroughly clean all the components.

2. Cut the cucumber, green apple, celery stalks, kale or spinach leaves, and peeled lemon into smaller pieces.

3. Utilizing a cold-press juicer, juice each ingredient separately.

4. To ensure that the juice is as fresh and nutrient-rich as possible, thoroughly stir it before drinking.

2. Orange-Rot Splash

This juice is a popular mix of fresh, organic fruits and veggies that is high in vitamins, minerals, and antioxidants.

Carrots have a lot of vitamin A, which is good for your eyes and your nervous system. Oranges have a lot of vitamin C, which is good for the nervous system and can help protect against damage from free radicals. Lemons also have a lot of vitamin C and are thought to have alkalizing qualities that can help keep the pH levels in the body in balance. Ginger is a root that is known to help with digestion and reduce inflammation.

When put together in a drink, these ingredients can help the immune system, aid digestion, and reduce inflammation, among other health benefits. It's important to always use fresh, organic products and to make the juice with a machine that keeps as many nutrients and enzymes as possible.

• Ingredients:

• Four carrots

(2) two oranges, peeled

• 1 peeled lemon

• An optional 1-inch slice of ginger

• Directions:

Thoroughly clean the carrots, oranges, lemon, and ginger (if using).

1. Smaller carrot chunks should be cut.

2. Utilizing a cold-press juicer, combine the juice of the carrots, oranges, lemon, and ginger.

3. Drink the juice after giving it a good stir.

4. Consume right away to get your day off to a revitalizing and refreshing start.

3. Beet-Apple-Carrot Juice

This juice is composed of fresh, organic beets, carrots, and apples. For more taste and health benefits, ginger may also be added.

- **Ingredients**:

- 1 medium-sized beetroot

- Three carrots

- 1 apple

- An optional 1-inch slice of ginger

- **Directions**:

Thoroughly wash the apple, carrots, beets, and ginger (if using).

1. Apple, carrots, and beets should all be cut into tiny pieces.

2. Use a cold-press juicer to combine the beets, carrots, apple, and ginger into juice.

3. To feel the juice's invigorating effects, thoroughly stir it before drinking.

Enjoy making one of these stimulating and delicious juices as part of your morning ritual.

4. Ginger Carrot Energizer

The carrots and ginger in this Carrot Ginger Energizer give out a burst of natural sweetness, while the ginger gives it a zingy kick. It's a fantastic alternative for a jolting morning beverage

- **Ingredients**:

- Four carrots

- A peeled 1-inch piece of ginger

- **Directions**:

1. Thoroughly wash the ginger and carrots.

2. Smaller carrot chunks should be cut.

3. Utilizing a cold-press juicer, combine the juice of the carrots and ginger.

4. Drink the juice after giving it a good stir.

5. For a revitalizing start to your day, sip on the juice right away.

Use organic vegetables wherever possible, and speak with a doctor or someone who practices Gerson Therapy for individualized guidance and changes based on your particular requirements and health situation.

Chapter 2: Cleansing Green Juices

1. The Ultimate Detox :

Juice from "The Ultimate Detox" is loaded with hydrating cucumber and nutrient-rich vegetables, while the tanginess of lemon rounds out the flavor.

Ingredients:

• Two big cucumbers

• 2 celery stalks

• One tiny bunch of kale

• One tiny bunch of spinach

• 1 tangerine

- 1 peeled lemon

- **Directions**:

1. Thoroughly clean all the components.

2. Reduce the size of the cucumbers, celery, kale, spinach, green apple, and peeled lemon.

3. Utilizing a cold-press juicer, juice each ingredient separately.

4. To fully meld the flavors, thoroughly stir the juice.

5. Consume the juice right away for a potent detoxifying and purifying effect.

This mixture offers a revitalizing energy boost while supporting the body's cleansing procedures.

2. Green Elixir:

In the "Leafy Elixir" drink, cucumber, lemon, and kale are combined with the cleansing and moisturizing effects of kale and spinach. The flavor of this purifying juice is enhanced by the sweetness of the green apples.

- **Ingredients**:

- One huge cucumber

- One tiny bunch of kale

- One tiny bunch of spinach

- 2 green apples

- 1 peeled lemon

- **Directions:**
1. Thoroughly clean all the components.

2. Reduce the size of the cucumber, kale, spinach, green apples, and peeled lemon.

3. Utilizing a cold-press juicer, juice each ingredient separately.

4. Drink the juice after giving it a good stir.

5. To enjoy the juice as a nourishing and purifying green elixir, drink it right away.

Both of these green juices offer a concentrated serving of nutrients from leafy greens and other purifying components while supporting detoxification.

Chapter 3: Tonics for Health

1. Infrared Glow

The powerful anti-inflammatory effects of turmeric and ginger are combined with pineapple's sweet, tropical flavor in the Golden Glow tonic. This tonic can provide the body a revitalizing boost while supporting its natural healing processes.

Ingredients:

- A peeled 1-inch piece of turmeric

- A peeled 1-inch piece of ginger

- 1 cup of chunks of fresh pineapple.

14

• Directions:

1. Thoroughly wash the pineapple, ginger, and turmeric.

2. Slice the pineapple, ginger, and turmeric into smaller pieces.

3. Use a cold-press juicer to combine the pineapple, ginger, and turmeric into one juice.

4. To ensure that all the tastes are blended, thoroughly stir the juice.

5. The tonic's anti-inflammatory qualities and refreshing flavor should be consumed right away.

2. Immunity Booster

The digestive advantages of fennel, the calming effects of aloe vera, and the cooling characteristics of mint are all combined in the Digestive Soother tonic.

You can drink on this tonic slowly to help digestion and ease digestive discomfort.

- **Ingredients:**

- Four oranges, peeled

- 1 serving strawberries

- 1 peeled lemon

- **Directions:**

1. Thoroughly wash the strawberries, lemon, and oranges.

2. Oranges, strawberries, and lemons should all be cut into smaller pieces.

3. Using a cold-press juicer, combine the orange, strawberry, and lemon juice.

4. To fully meld the flavors, thoroughly stir the juice.

5. To give your immune system a vitamin C-packed boost, consume the tonic right away.

The immune-supportive qualities of vitamin C, which is abundant in the Immune Booster tonic, are well established. A tart and revitalizing tonic made of oranges, strawberries, and lemon can help boost the immune system.

3. Stomach Soother:

• **Ingredients**:

- 1 cup pure, unadulterated aloe vera juice

- 4-5 fresh leaves of mint

- One tablespoon of fennel seeds

Directions:

1. Thoroughly wash the mint leaves.

2. To unleash their flavors, use a mortar and pestle to crush the mint leaves and fennel seeds.

3. Crushed mint leaves, fennel seeds, and aloe vera juice should all be put in a glass.

4. All the components should be thoroughly mixed.

5. To calm the digestive system, sip the tonic slowly.

Remember to modify the components and amounts according to your specific tastes.

Chapter 3: Elixirs of Restoratives,

1. Fruit Blast:

The Berry Blast drink has beets' purifying properties in addition to the antioxidant power of mixed berries. It gives off a delicious flavor explosion and may promote general health and wellbeing.

- **Ingredients**:

- One cup of mixed berries, including strawberries, blueberries, and raspberries

- 1 small, peeled beet

- **Directions**:

1. Thoroughly wash the beet and berries.

2. Reduce the size of the beet.

3. Use a cold-press juicer to combine the beet and mixed berries into juice.

4. To fully meld the flavors, thoroughly stir the juice.

5. To benefit from the elixir's antioxidant-rich benefits of berries and the purifying qualities of beets, drink it right away.

2. The Liver Love elixir

To assist liver health and detoxification, the Liver Love elixir was created specifically. A revitalizing elixir made from beets, carrots, and apples can support liver health and general energy.

• **Ingredients**:

• 1 small, peeled beet

- Two carrots

- 2 apples in green

- **Directions**:

1. Thoroughly wash the apples, carrots, and beets.

2. Apples, carrots, and beets should all be cut into smaller pieces.

3. Use a cold-press juicer to combine the beet, carrots, and apples into juice.

4. Drink the juice after giving it a good stir.

5. To take advantage of the liver-cleansing effects of beets and the nourishing effects of carrots and apples, consume the elixir right away.

3. Tropical Heaven

The tropical tastes of papaya, mango, and coconut water in the Tropical Paradise elixir provide a hydrated and invigorating experience. It offers necessary nutrients and can support electrolyte replacement.

- **Ingredients**:

- slices of ripe papaya

- slices of ripe mango

Coconut water, 1 cup

- **Directions:**

1. The papaya and mango should be peeled and the seeds taken out.

2. Mango and papaya should be cut into smaller pieces.

3. To a blender, add the papaya, mango, and coconut water.

4. Blend everything thoroughly until it's smooth.

5. Enjoy the flavors of the tropical paradise after pouring the elixir into a glass.

Remember to modify the components and amounts according to your specific tastes, and seek out individualized advice from a medical professional or Gerson Therapy practitioner.

4. Digestive Soother:

Aloe vera is a plant that looks like a cactus and has been used as a medicine for hundreds of years. It has anti-inflammatory chemicals in it that could help with digestive problems like irritable bowel syndrome (IBS) and acid reflux.

Overall, these three ingredients work together to possibly help with digestion and make digestion better as a whole. But it's important to remember that natural treatments like Digestive Soother might not work for everyone. Before trying any new supplement, it's always best to talk to a doctor.

Ingredients

- Aloe vera,
- mint,
- and fennel

Direction:

1. Cut the aloe vera leaf open,
2. Then scoop out the gel.
3. Mix fennel and mint in the juice.
4. Stir thoroughly, then sip right away.

Chapter 4: Recipes for Heart Health:

1. Beetroot-Celery Juice

Beetroot-celery juice is a type of vegetable drink made by blending or juicing beets, celery, and lemon together. Each of these things is good for your health in its own way.

Together, the beetroot and celery in the juice can help to support your health and fitness as a whole. The juice is thought to have anti-inflammatory, detoxifying, and energizing qualities. It may be especially helpful to foster healthy digestion, enhancing circulation, and reducing inflammation in the body.

Ingredients:

1. 2 beets,

2. 4 celery stalks,

3 1 peeled lemon,

Instructions:

1. Clean the beets and peel them.

2. Cut them up so they are smaller.

3. Put the beetroots and celery in a cold-press juicer and extract the juice.

4. Add the lemon to the juicer and blend it well.

5. Drink the juice as soon as you can.

2. Watermelon-mint juice:

Overall, drinking watermelon-mint juice is a tasty way to stay hydrated and get more vitamins and antioxidants. It could be especially helpful when it's hot outside or after you work out and you need to replace fluids and nutrients that you lost through sweat. But it's important to remember that fruit juice, which includes watermelon-mint juice, can be high in natural sugars, so it's best to drink it in moderation as part of a healthy diet.

Ingredients:

1. chunks of watermelon,

2. a quarter cup of fresh mint leaves,

3. and a peeled lemon.

4. two cups of fresh

Direction

1. Put the watermelon and mint in a cold-press juicer and get the juice out.

2. Put the lemon in the juicer and mix it together well.

3. Drink the juice as soon as possible.

Chapter 5: How to Cook for Healthy Kidneys

1. Cucumber-parsley juice:

Ingredients

1. two cucumbers,

2. a cup of fresh parsley leaves,

3. and a lemon that has been peeled.

Direction

1. Clean the cucumbers and cut them into smaller pieces.

2. Use a cold-press juicer to get the juice from the cucumbers and parsley.

3. Put the lemon in the juicer and mix it together well.

4. Drink the juice as soon as possible.

2. . Carrot, celery, and parsley juice:

Cucumber-parsley juice is made by mixing or juicing two cucumbers, a cup of fresh parsley leaves, and a lemon that has been peeled. This drink is a great way to stay hydrated and is full of nutrients that are good for your health and well-being as a whole.

Ingredients

1. four carrots,

2. two celery stalks,

3. one cup of fresh parsley leaves,

4. and one lemon that has been peeled.

Direction

1. Wash the carrots and peel them.

2. Cut the parts smaller.

3. Use a cold-press juicer to get the juice from the carrots, celery, and parsley.

4. Put the lemon in the juicer and mix it together well.

5. Drink the juice as soon as possible.

Chapter 6: Recipes for losing weight:

1. Apple-Cucumber Juice:

Apple-cucumber juice is made by mixing or juicing two green apples, one cucumber, and one peeled lemon. This drink is a great way to stay hydrated and is full of nutrients that are good for your health and well-being as a whole.

Together, these ingredients make a delicious and healthy juice that can help keep your digestive system healthy, boost your immune system, and give you a variety of important vitamins and antioxidants. But, as with any food or supplement, effects may vary from person to person, and it's always a good idea to talk to a doctor before making big changes to your diet or lifestyle.

Ingredients

1. Two green apples,

2. one cucumber,

3. and one lemon that has been removed.

Direction

1. Wash the apples and cucumbers, then cut them into smaller pieces.

2. Put the items in a cold-press juicer and get the juice out of them.

3. Put the lemon in the juicer and mix it together well.

4. Drink the juice as soon as possible.

2. Spinach, cucumber, and lemon juice:

Spinach, cucumber, and lemon juice is a type of vegetable juice made by blending or juicing one cup of spinach, one cucumber, and one peeled lemon. This juice is a great source of hydration and is packed with nutrients that can support overall health and well-being.

Together, these ingredients make a tasty and nutritious juice that can help promote healthy digestion, support immune function, and provide a range of important vitamins and antioxidants. However, as with any dietary supplement or food, individual results may vary, and it's always a good idea to consult with a healthcare provider before making significant changes to your diet or lifestyle.

Ingredients

1. one cup of spinach,

2. one cucumber,

3. and one lemon that has been peeled.

Direction

1. Wash the spinach and onion, then cut them into smaller pieces.

2. Put the items in a cold-press juicer and get the juice out of them.

3. Put the lemon in the juicer and mix it together well.

4. Drink the juice as soon as possible.

Chapter 7: Recipes for anti-Aging

1. Pomegranate-Carrot Juice:

Ingredients:

1. 1 cup of fresh pomegranate seeds,

2. 4 carrots,

3. 1 peeled lemon,

Directions:

1. Wash the carrots and peel them.

2. Cut the parts smaller.

3. Put the seeds and carrots in a cold-press juicer and get the juice out.

4. Put the lemon in the juicer and mix it together well.

5. Drink the juice as soon as possible.

2. Blueberry-Kale Juice:

Ingredients:

1. 1 cup of fresh blueberries,

2. 4 kale leaves,

3. 1 peeled lemon,

Directions:

1. Clean the kale and cut it into smaller pieces.

2. Put the kale and blueberries in a cold-press juicer and get the juice out.

3. Put the lemon in the juicer and mix it together well.

4. Drink the juice as soon as possible.

Chapter 8: Recipes for Healthy Brains:

1. Ginger-Turmeric Carrot Juice:

Ginger-turmeric carrot juice is made from fresh carrots, ginger root, turmeric root, and lemon. It is healthy and tastes good. Ginger and turmeric are renowned for their anti-inflammatory qualities and possible advantages for health, while carrots are full of vitamins and antioxidants. The lemon makes the juice taste tangy and fresh.

Ingredients

1. You'll need four carrots,

2. one inch of ginger root,

3. one inch of turmeric root,

4. and one peeled lemon.

Direction

1. Wash the carrots and peel them.

2. Cut the parts smaller.

3. Put the carrots, turmeric, and ginger in a cold-press juicer and get the juice out.

4. Put the lemon in the juicer and mix it together well.

5. Drink the juice as soon as possible.

2. Blueberry-Beetroot Juice:

Blueberry-beetroot juice is made from fresh blueberries, beets, and lemon. It is healthy and tastes great. Blueberries have a lot of antioxidants and may help the brain work better and prevent inflammation. Beets are also full of antioxidants, which can help lower blood pressure and improve athletic efficiency. Lemon gives the drink a sour taste and it's also great for your health. In general, drinking this juice is a great way to improve your health and give you more energy.

Ingredients

1. You'll need one cup of fresh blueberries,

2. two beets, and one peeled lemon.

Direction

1. Wash the beets and peel them.

2. Cut the parts smaller.

3. Put the beets and blueberries in a cold-press juicer and get the juice out.

4. Put the lemon in the juicer and mix it together well.

5. Drink the juice as soon as possible.

Chapter 9: Recipes for Anti-Cancer:

1. Carrot-Apple-Beet Juice:

Carrot-apple-beet juice is made from fresh carrots, green apples, beets, and lemon. It is healthy and delicious. Carrots are full of vitamins and enzymes, and green apples give the juice a sweet and sour taste and a lot of fiber. Beets are full of antioxidants, which help lower blood pressure and boost athletic ability.

Ingredients:

1. Two carrots,

2. One green apple,

3. One beet,

4. and one peeled lemon .

Direction

1. Wash the carrots and beets and peel them.

2. Cut the parts smaller.

3. Put the carrots, apple, and beets in a cold-press juicer and get the juice out.

4. Put the lemon in the juicer and mix it together well.

5. Drink the juice as soon as possible.

2. Grapefruit-Carrot Juice:

Some foods and drinks, like grapefruit-carrot juice, may be good for your health as a whole and may even lower your risk of getting cancer.

Grapefruit-carrot juice is full of strong antioxidants, vitamins, and minerals that may help keep cells and DNA from getting damaged, which can lead to cancer.

1. Two grapefruits,

2. Four carrots,

3. and one peeled lemon are the ingredients.

• **How to do it:**

1. Wash the carrots and oranges and peel them.

2. Cut the parts smaller.

3. Put the carrots and grapefruits in a cold-press juicer and squeeze out the juice.

4. Put the lemon in the juicer and mix it together well.

5. Drink the juice as soon as possible.

These juice ideas are simple to make at home and can be good for your health in different ways. Always use fresh vegetables and a juicer that keeps as many nutrients and enzymes as possible. Enjoy!

I hope that anyone who is doing Gerson Therapy will find these juice recipes helpful. Always use fresh, organic food and a machine that keeps as many nutrients and enzymes as possible.

Chapter 10: Juicing's significance in the Gerson Therapy

Juicing is a key component of the Gerson Therapy, a complementary medical strategy created by Dr. Max Gerson for the management and treatment of a variety of chronic conditions, including cancer. Juicing is regarded as a crucial part of this therapy for a number of reasons:

1. Freshly squeezed fruit and vegetable juices are a great source of vitamins, minerals, enzymes, and phytochemicals. Juicing makes it possible to consume these nutrients in concentrated form, giving the body a high degree of nourishment that is bioavailable. The immune system, cellular healing, and general health are supported by this.

2. Juicing aids in increasing fluid intake, which promotes hydration. Supporting different biological processes, such as digestion, detoxification, and nutrition absorption, requires adequate hydration. Patients undergoing the Gerson Therapy can make sure they are well hydrated by ingesting freshly squeezed juices.

3. The Gerson Therapy places a strong emphasis on preserving an alkaline environment in the body since it is thought to promote healing and slow the proliferation of cancer cells. Green juices are particularly alkalizing and can help balance the pH levels in the body because they are made from fresh vegetables.

4. The Gerson Therapy is primarily focused on assisting the body's own detoxifying mechanisms. Juicing reduces the stress on the digestive system and gives the body nutrients and enzymes that are easily absorbed, which aids in detoxifying. It enables the body to focus its attention on removing impurities and encouraging healing.

5. **Support for the liver:** The Gerson Therapy places a strong emphasis on liver detoxification. Juices that contain ingredients that improve liver function and encourage detoxification include carrot and beet juice. The liver's capacity to break down and get rid of toxins from the body can be improved with the aid of these fluids.

6. **Increased Antioxidant Intake:** The abundance of antioxidants in fresh juices helps to shield the body from oxidative stress and free radical damage. In the context of the Gerson Therapy, antioxidants are essential for lowering inflammation, boosting the immune system, and minimizing cellular damage.

7. Juicing enables the digestive system to recover and take a break. Juices that have just been freshly squeezed allow the body to absorb nutrients faster and with less effort. People with impaired digestive function, which is common in many chronic conditions, may benefit from this.

8. Raw juices contain natural enzymes that can support the body's general enzyme activity and help with digestion.

Enzymes are essential for many biological functions, including the digestion of food and the absorption of nutrients. Juices high in enzymes are a key component of the Gerson Therapy because they promote efficient nutrient absorption and digestion.

9. **Variety of Nutrients**: Juicing enables a wide range of fruits and vegetables to be used in the treatment. Patients can gain from a wide variety of vitamins, minerals, and phytonutrients by combining various food products with different nutritional profiles in juices. This aids in offering a wide range of nutrients required for promoting the body's healing processes.

10. **Caloric Restriction**: In order to promote the body's natural healing and cleansing processes, the Gerson Therapy often entails caloric restriction. When opposed to eating entire foods, juicing offers a concentrated supply of nutrients while ingesting less calories. In some circumstances, if calorie moderation is required, this strategy may be effective.

11. **Palatability:** For those undergoing the Gerson Therapy, consuming a lot of fruits and vegetables can be difficult. Consuming more plant-based food in a more appetizing form is made simpler by juicing. This can increase therapy compliance and guarantee a steady intake of important nutrients.

12. **Support for the Emotions**: Patients who juice may have improved psychological well-being. Fresh, vivid juice preparation and consumption may be upbeat and powerful. It promotes taking a preventative approach to health and can make people feel more invested in their healing process.

Although the Gerson Therapy has become more well-known, keep in mind that it is still regarded as an alternative therapy, and whether or not it is useful for particular illnesses is still up for discussion. If you want to know if the Gerson Therapy is right for you, you must speak with a trained medical expert or a Gerson Therapy practitioner. They can offer individualized direction and supervision during the course of the therapy.

Chapter 11: Advantages of Gerson Therapy

Due to the unique ingredient combinations used in Gerson Therapy juice recipes, various possible advantages exist. The advantages of the juice recipes employed in the Gerson Therapy include the following:

1. The use of fresh, organic fruits and vegetables that are high in vital vitamins, minerals, enzymes, and phytochemicals is emphasized in Gerson Therapy juice recipes. The juices contain a robust supply of bioavailable nutrition due to the high concentration of these components, supporting the body's healing and regeneration processes.

2. Apples, carrots, beets, leafy greens, and other antioxidant-rich foods are frequently used in the Gerson Therapy's juice recipes. Free radicals and oxidative stress, which can contribute to chronic diseases and quicken aging, are both combatted by antioxidants. People receiving the Gerson Therapy can increase their antioxidant intake and boost general cellular health by frequently ingesting these juices.

3. Alkalizing Properties: Many juice recipes from the Gerson Therapy are created to assist the body become more alkaline. Alkaline veggies including celery, cucumber, and leafy greens are frequently used in these recipes. It is thought that bringing the body's pH level down inhibits the development and spread of cancer cells as well as other chronic illnesses.

4. promote for Natural Detoxification Processes: The Gerson Therapy strives to promote the body's natural detoxification processes, and the juice recipes are a key component of this goal. Green leafy vegetables like spinach and kale are among the ingredients known for their cleansing qualities. These juices can enhance the body's detoxification process by enhancing liver function.

5. Gerson Therapy juice recipes offer a revitalizing and replenishing source of liquids, which will help you stay hydrated. For proper cellular operation, digestion, and toxin removal, one must maintain good hydration. The juice recipes make it easier to stay properly hydrated, especially for people who might have trouble drinking enough water or having trouble digesting food.

6. **Support for Digestion:** Gerson Therapy juice recipes are made to be easily digested and provide nutrients in a form that the body can easily absorb. Individuals with impaired digestive function or those who are having digestive problems can get comfort from the juices. The juices stimulate the digestive system and encourage healing by supplying vital nutrients without the need for protracted digestion.

7. **Variety and Flavor**: The Gerson Therapy juice recipes use a variety of fruits and vegetables, resulting in a wide range of flavors and nutritional profiles. This variety makes juice use more enjoyable and sustainable as a long-term nutritional

approach, helping treatment patients maintain interest in and enjoyment from their daily juice intake.

8. **Support for the immunological System:** The Gerson Therapy's nutrient-rich juices significantly strengthen the immunological system. The vitamins, minerals, and antioxidants in the juices promote the body's defensive mechanisms against infections, illnesses, and chronic diseases by boosting the immunological response.

9. **Many of the constituents in Gerson Therapy juice recipes**, including turmeric, ginger, and leafy greens, have anti-inflammatory effects. Consuming these anti-inflammatory juices may help reduce inflammation and boost general wellbeing because chronic inflammation is a common contributing factor to many disorders.

10. The juice recipes for the Gerson Therapy are created to support healing and cellular repair. The body receives an abundance of nutrients, especially from organic fruits and vegetables, which give it the building blocks it needs to mend damaged tissues, boost organ function, and speed up recovery in general.

11. **Better Bowel Movements:** Juice recipes for the Gerson Therapy frequently include substances that have natural laxative effects, like prunes or aloe vera. These juices can aid in enhancing bowel motions and reducing constipation, which is a significant worry for patients receiving the medication.

Promoting regular bowel motions is essential for the body to effectively detoxify and eliminate waste.

12. Gerson Therapy juice recipes typically have low calorie counts and high fiber content, which can help with healthy weight management. The drinks provide a balanced food intake while offering satisfaction and nourishment. Additionally, by adhering to the Gerson Therapy's all-encompassing strategy, which entails food adjustments and lifestyle adjustments, people may eventually reach a healthier body weight.

13. **Emotional and Psychological Benefits**: Using Gerson Therapy juice recipes to prepare and consume can have a favorable emotional and psychological impact. A sense of empowerment, well-being, and hope can be enhanced by taking an active role in one's health, engaging in therapy, and nourishing the body with vibrant, fresh juices.

It's crucial to keep in mind that the Gerson Therapy is an alternative method and should only be used under the supervision of a licensed healthcare provider. To ensure safety and efficacy, they can offer tailored suggestions, track development, and modify the therapy as necessary.

Chapter 12: Appropriate Juicing Methods and Tools

A key element of the Gerson Therapy is juicing, and for the therapy to be as effective as possible, knowing the right methods and having the right tools are essential. In the context of the Gerson Therapy, this chapter focuses on the important factors to take into account during juicing.

1. Choosing the Best Gear:

a. Cold-Press Juicer: According to the Gerson Therapy, you should use a hydraulic press or a two-step juicer that uses a grinding or masticating action before hydraulic pressing. Juice is extracted using pressure rather than heat in cold-press juicers, which helps maintain the juice's essential nutrients and enzymes.

2. Produce preparation:

a. **Choose organic produce**: It is crucial to utilize organic fruits and vegetables to reduce exposure to pesticides and other toxins. The usage of organic food is heavily encouraged by the Gerson Therapy to aid the body's healing process.

b. **Washing**: To eliminate dirt, debris, and any lingering pesticide residue, wash all fruits and vegetables very well before juicing.

c. **Peeling and Pitting**: Before juicing, some fruits, such as citrus fruits, may need to be peeled. To avoid bitterness or potential toxicity, remove any seeds or pits from fruits.

3. **Technique for juicing**:

a. Cut the fruits and vegetables properly so that they may easily fit into the feeding funnel of the juicer. This keeps clogs at bay and improves the juicing procedure.

b. Ingredients that are Balanced: Use the juice recipes that the Gerson Therapy or your healthcare provider recommends. For therapeutic purposes, these recipes have been specifically created to offer the ideal nutrient balance.

c. Follow the suggested order for juicing the components. You can alternate between leafy greens and soft fruits like apples or pears to make juicing easier and increase yield.

4. **Juice Consumption and Storage**:

a. **Immediate Consumption**: It is best to consume the freshly squeezed juice right away after juicing in order to retain the most nutrients.

b. Juice should be transferred into a glass container with an airtight lid and refrigerated if it needs to be kept for a brief period of time.

To reduce nutritional loss, consume the juice within 24-48 hours.

c. **Avoid Oxidation**: Fill the juice container to the brim to avoid contact with air, which will lessen oxidation and nutrient deterioration. Before sealing the container, think about using a vacuum sealer or mixing in a little lemon juice with the liquid.

5. **Cleaning and upkeep**:

a. Refer to the juicer's instruction booklet for proper cleaning and maintenance instructions. Follow the manufacturer's instructions. There may be particular guidelines for each juicer.

b. **Prompt Cleaning**: To avoid residue accumulation and maintain peak efficiency, clean the juicer right away after use.

c. **Complete Cleaning**: Take apart the juicer and gently wash each component in warm, soapy water. Pay close attention to the juicing screen because pulp and other debris might collect there.

6. **Volume and Frequency**:

a. **Recommended Daily Intake**: A major component of the Gerson Therapy is ingesting a lot of freshly squeezed juice. To ensure that you are consuming the right amount and frequency of juice for your particular condition, it is crucial to adhere to the recommendations made by your doctor or Gerson Therapy practitioner.

b. Gradual Increase: It is advised to start with lower amounts of juice and gradually increase the amount over time if you are new to juicing or the Gerson Therapy. This enables your body to adapt to the higher nutrient intake.

7. **Utilization of pulp**:

a. **Composting**: You can use the pulp left behind after juicing to improve the soil in your garden. This encourages sustainability and reduces waste.

b. **Pulp reuse**: In some situations, the pulp can be used in baking, soup, or broth recipes. To save waste and utilize the product to its full potential, experiment with adding the pulp to different meals.

8. **Other advice:**

a. **Rotate Ingredients**: To provide a varied variety of nutrients and guard against potential sensitivities or allergies, it is good to rotate the fruits and vegetables you use in your juices.

b. **Monitor Reactions**: Keep track of how your body reacts to certain fluids. Consult your doctor or a Gerson Therapy practitioner for modifications if you have any negative reactions or sensitivities.

c. **Proper Chewing**: It is advised to swish the juice around in your mouth before swallowing to aid with digestion. Saliva includes digestive enzymes, thus this enables the juice to combine with it.

9. **Seek Direction**: a. Support from a healthcare professional: Juicing is only one component of the Gerson Therapy, which is a holistic therapeutic approach. Working closely with an experienced healthcare expert or Gerson Therapy practitioner who can offer advice, track your development, and make any required modifications to your juicing routine is essential.

.

Chapter 13: Adding Gerson Therapy Juices to Your Routine

Juices from the Gerson Therapy might be a helpful addition to your regimen for supporting your health and wellbeing. You can incorporate Gerson Therapy drinks into your everyday routine by following these tips:

1. Decide on specified times throughout the day to consume your juices as part of the Gerson Therapy. By doing this, you may create a schedule and make sure you always include the juices in your day.

2. Plan ahead and set aside time to make the juice. To prepare the fruits and vegetables for your Gerson Therapy juices, set aside a dedicated time each day to wash, chop, and juice them. You'll always have fresh juices on hand this way when you need them.

3. Store your newly made juices properly by placing them in the refrigerator in airtight bottles, ideally made of glass. The freshness and nutritional integrity of the juices are kept up by proper storage.

4. **Drink very Away:** To enhance the nutritional value of Gerson Therapy juices, it is preferable to drink them very away after preparation. Juices that have just been made from scratch have the highest concentration of enzymes and nutrients.

5. Include a range of Gerson Therapy juice recipes in your regimen because variation is important. Try with various fruit and vegetable combinations to make your juices more flavorful and fascinating.

6. When at all feasible, look for organic produce when buying produce for juicing. In accordance with the tenets of the Gerson Therapy, organic produce is grown without the use of artificial pesticides and chemicals.

7.Pay attention to how your body reacts to the juices used in the Gerson Therapy. Keep track of any alterations or enhancements to your health and wellbeing. Consult your healthcare provider if you have any worries or queries.

9. **Start Slowly**: If you're new to Gerson Therapy juices, begin by introducing one or two juices into your daily schedule. As you get more accustomed to it, you can progressively add more. This enables your body to adapt to the higher nutrient intake.

10. Make a list of the components needed for your Gerson Therapy juices to help you plan your purchasing. To guarantee that you have a constant supply of fresh vegetables on hand, plan your shopping visits in advance.

11. **Batch preparation**: When making Gerson Therapy juices, think about making bigger batches ahead of time, especially for busier days. Although you can keep them in the

fridge for up to 24 to 48 hours, you should be aware that the nutritious content may gradually decrease.

12. **Make It Fun:** Adding variation to your concoctions and experimenting with various flavors will make drinking Gerson Therapy juices more fun. Don't be scared to alter the recipes to suit your personal tastes.

13. **Include Rituals:** Establish a tranquil, designated area in which to consume your Gerson Therapy juices. This might assist you in viewing the ingestion of juice as a healing and mindful exercise.

14. **Drinking Water Between Juices**: Along with the Gerson Therapy juices, keep in mind to drink plenty of clean, fresh water all day long. Maintaining proper hydration helps the body remove toxins and maintains overall wellness.

15. **Track Your Progress**: During your Gerson Therapy journey, keep a notebook to record your juice intake, any changes in your symptoms or general wellbeing, and any observations you make. This will enable you to keep tabs on your development and, if necessary, make changes.

16. Connect with people who are utilizing the Gerson Therapy or sign up for support groups online or in person to seek help. On your path to recovery, exchanging stories, tips, and recipes can inspire and support you.

Keep in mind that the juices are but one component of the Gerson Therapy, which is a comprehensive therapeutic approach. It is crucial to adhere to all instructions given by a medical professional or Gerson Therapy practitioner.

Chapter 14: Establishing a Daily Juice Routine Is Covered

Creating A Daily Juice Routine

Making juicing a regular part of your routine might be made easier if you create a daily schedule for it. You can create a schedule by following the procedures listed below:

1. **Decide on the number of juices you'll drink each day as part of the Gerson Therapy**. This may change depending on your individual requirements and the advice of your doctor or Gerson Therapy practitioner.

2. **Pick the Best Times**: When deciding when to drink your juice, take into account your daily schedule. In order to ensure a continuous intake of nutrients, you should ideally spread them out throughout the day. Having juice in the morning, mid-morning, afternoon, and evening is beneficial to many people.

3. **Allocate Time for Preparation**: Calculate how much time you'll need to get your juices ready. This entails washing, chopping, and juicing the produce, as well as cleaning the juicer afterwards. Schedule enough time so that you won't feel rushed as you perform these duties.

4. **Establish a Juicing Routine**: Use your selected juice schedule to determine particular times for juicing. You may set aside 15-20 minutes in the morning, for instance, to make

and drink your first juice. Create a schedule that suits you best and follow it religiously.

5. **Plan Your Shopping**: To make sure you have a sufficient supply of fresh vegetables for juicing, plan your grocery shopping visits in advance. To keep a stock of fruits and vegetables, think about preparing a shopping plan and setting aside time for frequent trips to the grocery store or farmers' market.

6. **If your schedule is hectic, think about preparing part of your ingredients in advance**. Your fruits and vegetables should be washed and chopped the night before so they are ready to be juiced in the morning. This can help you save time and streamline the juicing process.

7. **Set Reminders:** If necessary, use a calendar app, set reminders or alarms on your phone, or both to remember you when it's time to drink your juice. This can assist you in maintaining your juicing regimen, particularly in the beginning.

8. **Maintain Flexibility**: Setting up a routine is helpful, but it's also crucial to remain adaptable and flexible as necessary. Don't worry if you can't stick to your exact juicing routine on some days because life can get in the way. Simply modify your plans accordingly, then resume your juicing regimen the next day.

Keep in mind that the Gerson Therapy is a unique treatment procedure, so it's crucial to adhere to the instructions given by a healthcare provider or certified Gerson Therapy practitioner. On the precise timing and frequency of your juice consumption, they can make tailored recommendations.

Chapter 11: Suggestions for Buying Organic Food

As part of its mission to reduce exposure to artificial chemicals and pesticides, the Gerson Therapy emphasizes the importance of buying organic fruit. Here are some hints to assist you in locating and obtaining organic produce:

1. **Local Farmers' Markets**: Visit your neighborhood farmers' markets to meet up with nearby growers of organic food in person. They offer a huge selection of fresh, organic fruits and vegetables as well as information on their farming methods.

2. **Join a local CSA program. Community Supported Agriculture (CSA).** Through CSA programs, you can sign up to get a regular portion of an area farm's organic produce. By doing this, you can get recently harvested organic produce while also assisting neighborhood farmers.

3. **Find local organic or health food stores by searching for them online.** You may frequently find a variety of organic fruits and vegetables at these stores' dedicated

organic areas. They might also stock specialized goods made just for juicing.

4. **Online delivery of organic groceries**: A lot of online supermarket delivery businesses now include options for organic products. Find trustworthy websites that focus on organic and sustainably sourced food. If there aren't many farmers' markets or organic retailers nearby, this option can be more practical.

5. **Local Organic Farms:** Do some research on organic or conventional farms in the area. Pick-your-own alternatives are available on some farms, allowing you to go to the farm and gather your own organic produce. This offers a distinctive experience and guarantees the produce's freshness and quality.

6. **If you have the space and resources, think about growing your own organic fruits and veggies.** A tiny garden might be started, or you can grow food in pots or other containers. By doing so, you can guarantee that your food is organic and have total control over the growing process.

7. **When buying food from retailers, carefully study labels and certifications.** Look for organic certificates like the USDA Organic seal or the equivalent seal for your nation. These labels reveal that organic agricultural techniques were used to cultivate the produce.

8. **When purchasing produce, don't be afraid to inquire about the agricultural and sourcing methods.** To find out more about the organic foods they sell, talk to nearby farmers, store owners, or customer service personnel.

Although organic food is preferred, it may not always be accessible or economical. When this occurs, prioritize the produce on the "Dirty Dozen" list, which lists the produce with the highest pesticide levels, and think about purchasing organic versions. Produce on the "Clean Fifteen" list has lower pesticide residues and can be bought traditionally if necessary.

Chapter 15: Making and Preserving Juices for Ease of Use

You may maintain a regular juicing regimen by preparing and storing juices in a simple way. Here are some pointers for convenient juice preparation and storage:

1. **Prepare larger amounts of juice ahead of time by setting aside a specified window of time**. Depending on your tastes and schedule, you can do this either once or twice a day. To save time, wash, chop, and juice more fruits and vegetables at once.

2. **Airtight Containers:** To store your juices, use airtight glass bottles or containers. Juices are kept in glass containers to retain their quality and freshness while limiting exposure to light and air. To avoid oxidation, make sure the containers have tight-fitting lids.

3. **Fill Containers to the Brim:** To reduce air exposure when storing juices, fill the containers completely. As a result, the oxidation process is slowed down and the liquids' nutritious value is preserved.

4. **Refrigeration: To** keep your freshly made juices fresh, store them in the refrigerator. Juices typically retain their nutritional content when kept in the refrigerator for up to 24 to 48 hours. To maximize their freshness, it's ideal to eat them as soon as you can.

5. **Labeling:** Write the name of the juice and the date it was made on the outside of each container. By doing so, you can monitor the freshness of the juices and make sure you're drinking them in the right order.

6. Juices can be frozen for extended storage if you need to keep them for a longer period of time. Put the freshly made juice into freezer-safe containers or ice cube trays. Don't forget to leave room at the top for expansion during freezing. Juices that have been frozen can normally be kept for a few weeks.

7. **When a frozen juice is ready to be consumed, place it in the refrigerator the night before to allow it to defrost gradually.** As an alternative, you can hasten the thawing process by submerging the frozen juice container in a basin of ice water. Avoid thawing frozen foods in the microwave because doing so can reduce their nutritional value.

8. **Before consuming, shake or stir your juice because it could naturally split in storage.** Give the juice a vigorous shake or mix before drinking to make sure the nutrients are dispersed equally.

9. **Purchase leak-proof and transportable containers if you intend to carry your juices with you.** There are several options that make it simple for you to transport your juices, including stainless steel or glass bottles with silicone sleeves.

10. **Be Aware of Temperature Changes:** When transporting or storing juices, be aware of temperature changes. To keep your juices fresh and high-quality, keep them out of the sun, heat sources, and severe temperatures.

Always follow the correct food safety procedures, and throw away any juices that have been sitting around too long or show indications of deterioration.

You may readily prepare and store your Gerson Therapy juices by using the advice in this book, which will make it simpler for you to include them into your daily routine.

Here are some further suggestions for quickly preparing and preserving juices:

11. Control your portions by dividing your juices into smaller servings. If you prefer to consume juice in smaller, more regular amounts throughout the day, this may be useful. To measure out individual portions, use smaller glass bottles or containers.

12. **Juice Storage Bags:** Using juice storage bags created especially for holding liquids is another choice for practical storage. These bags often include a zip-lock seal to stop leakage and are BPA-free. When you're on the go, you may easily transport them in a backpack or cooler because they are lightweight.

13. **Juice Ice Cubes**: If you have extra juice that you won't use up within the advised storage period, think about freezing it in ice cube trays. Juice ice cubes can be added to smoothies or used to flavor water or other beverages in the future.

14. **Think about using juicing containers:** Some juicers come with unique containers that may be used to store the juice on-the-spot. These containers can be put directly in the refrigerator and frequently include airtight lids. To make the juicing process simpler, see if your juicer has compatible storage containers.

15. **Take Oxidation Precautions:** Vacuum sealing is one method you might use to reduce oxidation and maintain the freshness of your juices. The shelf life of your juices is increased by vacuum sealing because it eliminates extra air from the container, which slows oxidation.

16. **Planning ahead can ensure you have access to fresh juices while traveling or taking your juices somewhere else than your house**. To keep your juices kept and fresh throughout transit, think about taking a portable cooler bag or an insulated container.

17. Pre-cut **vegetables: You can pre-cut portions of your vegetables to save time during preparation.** For instance, wash and chop your leafy greens before putting them in the refrigerator in an airtight bag or sealed container.

When you're ready to juice, they will be available this manner.

Conclusion

In conclusion, Garson Therapy juice recipes have many advantages and are essential to this all-encompassing approach to healing. You may provide your body a concentrated amount of nutrients, enzymes, and antioxidants that can promote your general health and wellbeing by introducing fresh, organic juices into your daily routine.

The value of Gerson Therapy juice recipes rests in their capacity to deliver a strong dose of necessary vitamins, minerals, and phytonutrients that boost immune function, detoxification, cellular repair, and general vitality. These organic juices, which are produced from carefully chosen fruits and vegetables, can help the body become more alkaline, lessen inflammation, and encourage healing.

You are actively nourishing your body and promoting its natural healing processes by learning about the Gerson Therapy and incorporating juicing into your health journey. Many people who are looking for alternative methods of health and wellness have turned to Gerson Therapy, which has shown promising outcomes for a number of diseases.

Keep in mind that beginning any new therapy or treatment calls for dedication, tolerance, and direction from trained medical professionals or Gerson Therapy practitioners. They may offer you individualized guidance, keep track of your development, and make sure you adhere to the therapy in a safe and efficient manner.

Although adopting the Gerson Therapy and juicing into your lifestyle may present some problems, realize that you are making a significant decision for your health. Remind yourself of the potential advantages you may encounter on this trip to help you stay committed and motivated.

Find a friendly environment to live in or join a support group of people who have embraced the Gerson Therapy or other similar therapeutic modalities. Sharing your triumphs, setbacks, and experiences can inspire and support others as you go.

Above all, pay attention to your body, have faith in the process, and practice self-compassion. Every step you take toward adopting Gerson Therapy juice recipes into your life is a step toward better health since healing takes time.

I wish you luck as you embark on your Gerson Therapy and juicing journey. Remember that by making these healthy decisions, you are taking control of your health and giving your body the support it needs to cure itself.

And please do not forget to leave an honest review on Amazon if you find this book useful.

Remain blessed!

Made in United States
Troutdale, OR
01/02/2024

16645865R00046